Super Explorer's

PLANETS

Tamara Hartson

What is a Planet?

A planet is a spherical (round) body that orbits (circles) a star. Planets can be made of rock, gas or ice. Rocky planets are usually smaller than gas or gas and ice planets. Earth is a rocky planet.

A rogue planet is one that does not orbit a star. Rogue planets circle around the centre of the galaxy instead.

What is a Moon?

A moon is a rocky or icy body that orbits a planet. Some moons are spherical, but others are irregular. Moons are also called natural satellites.

Scientists think that planets are formed from the dust, debris and gas that circle a newly-formed star. Planets are created when dust and debris clump together. Eventually, larger and larger clumps collide to form a planet.

Gas and ice giants are usually very large. Gas giants are mostly hydrogen and helium. Ice planets have hydrogen and helium, but they also have water, ammonia and methane. Both types are believed to be solid at the center.

How Planets Form

Some planets may have rings surrounding them. Rings are thought to be the remains of the material and gas that formed the planet.

Our Solar System has 8 planets that circle around the Sun. Some planets have moons. Earth has one moon, and Jupiter has 69!

The eight planets showing their size differences and arranged in order: Mercury, Venus, Earth, Mars, Jupiter, Saturn, Uranus and Neptune.

Pluto was once thought to be a planet, but it is now called a dwarf planet, meaning it is too small to be seen as a true planet.

The Sun's gravity is what keeps all the planets circling around it.

Solar System

Mercury

LOCATION: First planet from the sun

TIME TO CIRCLE THE SUN: 88 days

NUMBER OF MOONS: 0

CAN HUMANS LIVE HERE: No

TIME FOR SUNLIGHT TO REACH THE PLANET: 3.2 minutes

DISTANCE FROM THE SUN: 57 million kilometers (average)
                                35 million miles (average)

AVERAGE SURFACE TEMPERATURE: Hot! (117 °C) (243 °F)

GRAVITY: Less than Earth. 45 kilograms (100 pounds)
  on Earth is 17 kilograms (38 pounds) on Mercury.

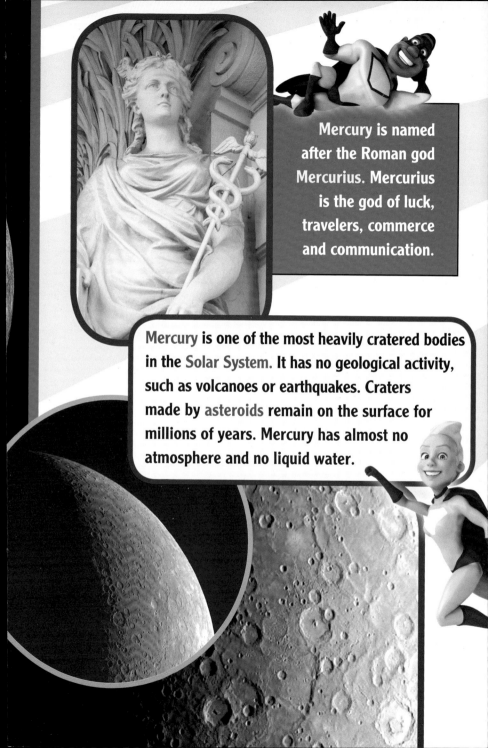

Mercury is named after the Roman god Mercurius. Mercurius is the god of luck, travelers, commerce and communication.

Mercury is one of the most heavily cratered bodies in the Solar System. It has no geological activity, such as volcanoes or earthquakes. Craters made by asteroids remain on the surface for millions of years. Mercury has almost no atmosphere and no liquid water.

Venus

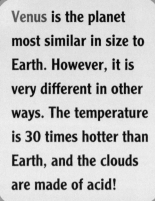

Venus **is the planet most similar in size to Earth. However, it is very different in other ways. The temperature is 30 times hotter than Earth, and the clouds are made of acid!**

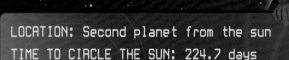

```
LOCATION: Second planet from the sun
TIME TO CIRCLE THE SUN: 224.7 days
NUMBER OF MOONS: 0
CAN HUMANS LIVE HERE: No
TIME FOR SUNLIGHT TO REACH THE PLANET: 6 minutes
DISTANCE FROM THE SUN: 108 million kilometers (average)
                       67 million miles (average)
AVERAGE SURFACE TEMPERATURE: Very hot! (462 °C) (863 °F)
GRAVITY: Similar to Earth. 45 kilograms (100 pounds)
    on Earth is 41 kilograms (91 pounds) on Venus.
```

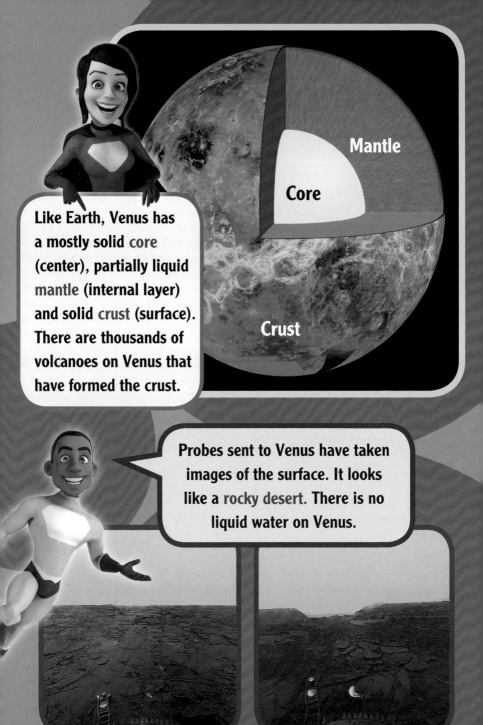

Mantle

Core

Crust

Like Earth, Venus has a mostly solid core (center), partially liquid mantle (internal layer) and solid crust (surface). There are thousands of volcanoes on Venus that have formed the crust.

Probes sent to Venus have taken images of the surface. It looks like a rocky desert. There is no liquid water on Venus.

Earth

LOCATION: Third planet from the sun

TIME TO CIRCLE THE SUN: 365 days

NUMBER OF MOONS: 1

CAN HUMANS LIVE HERE: Yes!

TIME FOR SUNLIGHT TO REACH THE PLANET: 8.3 minutes

DISTANCE FROM THE SUN: 150 million kilometers (average)
                      93 million miles (average)

AVERAGE SURFACE TEMPERATURE: Perfect! (15 °C) (59 °F)

Our Home

Earth is the fifth largest planet in the solar system. Most of Earth is covered by oceans. More than 8 million kinds of life live on Earth, including about 7 billion humans.

At night, city lights shine brightly and are visible from space. These night lights are around the world where people live in large numbers.

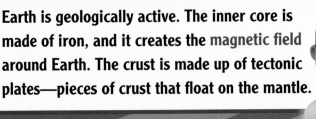

Earth is geologically active. The inner core is made of iron, and it creates the magnetic field around Earth. The crust is made up of tectonic plates—pieces of crust that float on the mantle.

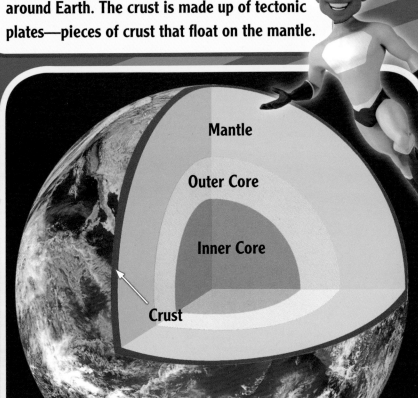

Mantle

Outer Core

Inner Core

Crust

Earth's magnetic field has enough pressure to block dangerous cosmic radiation, preventing it from reaching life on the surface.

Earth has one moon, called Luna. Our Moon is large and easy to see from Earth. The rise and fall of ocean tides on Earth are caused by the gravity of our Moon.

The Moon even has mountains—but they look very different from the mountains on Earth!

Man on the Moon

Humans cannot live on the Moon because there is no air. Astronauts have to wear special space suits with air tanks so they can breathe.

People have made 9 trips to the Moon. Each trip was called an Apollo Mission. In total, 12 astronauts have walked on the Moon. The Moon has less gravity than Earth, so walking on the Moon is like bouncing very slowly. You could easily jump as high as a 6-storey building!

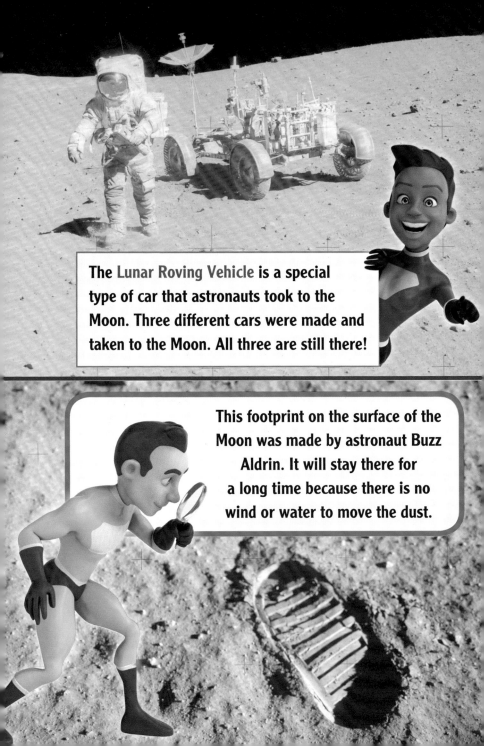

The **Lunar Roving Vehicle** is a special type of car that astronauts took to the Moon. Three different cars were made and taken to the Moon. All three are still there!

This footprint on the surface of the Moon was made by astronaut Buzz Aldrin. It will stay there for a long time because there is no wind or water to move the dust.

Mars

Mars has polar ice caps just like Earth.

LOCATION: Fourth planet from the sun

TIME TO CIRCLE THE SUN: 686.9 days

NUMBER OF MOONS: 2

CAN HUMANS LIVE HERE: No

TIME FOR SUNLIGHT TO REACH THE PLANET: 12.6 minutes

DISTANCE FROM THE SUN: 228 million kilometers (average)
           141 million miles (average)

AVERAGE SURFACE TEMPERATURE: Cold! (-63 °C) (-81 °F)

GRAVITY: Less than Earth. 45 kilograms (100 pounds)
   on Earth is 17 kilograms (38 pounds) on Mars.

Mars is the fourth planet in the Solar System. Mars is a rocky planet. It is different from Earth because it is smaller and doesn't have oceans. The air on Mars is thin and has little oxygen.

The surface of Mars looks like a rocky desert. The rocks have lots of iron, so the planet looks red. People often call Mars the Red Planet.

People have never been to Mars. Scientists are planning to build special spacecraft that one day may take astronauts to Mars.

Scientists have sent several rovers to Mars. Two of them are still sending information and photos back to Earth for researchers to study.

Rovers are like small cars that have computers and cameras. Before rovers are sent to Mars, they are built and tested here on Earth at special space research centres.

Mars Missions

The Surface of Mars

The Mars rover **Curiosity** took this selfie on the surface of Mars in 2013. We have learned a great deal about Mars from rock samples and photos the rovers have taken.

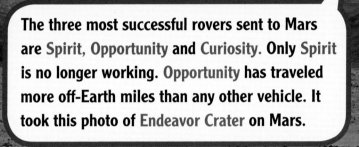

The three most successful rovers sent to Mars are Spirit, Opportunity and Curiosity. Only Spirit is no longer working. Opportunity has traveled more off-Earth miles than any other vehicle. It took this photo of Endeavor Crater on Mars.

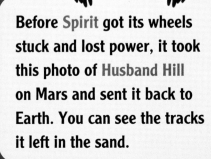

Before Spirit got its wheels stuck and lost power, it took this photo of Husband Hill on Mars and sent it back to Earth. You can see the tracks it left in the sand.

Moons of Mars

Mars has two moons. They are named Phobos and Deimos. Phobos is the larger moon, and it is closer to Mars. The closer a satellite is to a planet, the faster it has to move to stay in orbit. Phobos moves so fast that it rises and sets twice each Martian day.

Jupiter

Jupiter is the largest planet in our solar system. The Romans named this planet after their god Jupiter, the god of the sky. Jupiter is easy to see in the sky, it is the third brightest object after the Moon and Venus.

LOCATION: Fifth planet from the sun

TIME TO CIRCLE THE SUN: almost 12 years

NUMBER OF MOONS: 69

CAN HUMANS LIVE HERE: No

TIME FOR SUNLIGHT TO REACH THE PLANET: 43.2 minutes

DISTANCE FROM THE SUN: 228 million kilometers (average)
141 million miles (average)

AVERAGE SURFACE TEMPERATURE: Very cold! (-148 °C) (-234 °F)

GRAVITY: More than Earth. 45 kilograms (100 pounds)
on Earth is 115 kilograms (253 pounds) on Jupiter.

Jupiter has 69 moons! Most of Jupiter's moons have irregular shapes and are quite small. The four main moons are large and spherical. They are called the Galilean Moons.

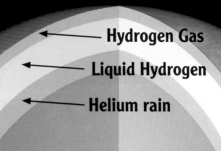

Hydrogen Gas ←

Liquid Hydrogen ←

Helium rain ←

Liquid Metallic Hydrogen

Rock & Ice Core ——→

Jupiter is a gas giant, which means it mostly made of hydrogen and helium. Gas giants are not entirely made of gas. Jupiter probably has a small, solid core surrounded by a layer of liquid metallic hydrogen.

This is the view of Jupiter's south pole. It is many different images pieced together and is the most detailed view of Jupiter's southern region that we have. The images were taken by the Cassini probe in the year 2000.

Did you know that Jupiter has rings? Unlike the rings of Saturn, Jupiter's rings are mostly made of dust and are faint. They are only visible with powerful telescopes or from space probes sent to Jupiter. There are 4 rings: Halo, Main Ring, Amalthea Gossamer Ring and Thebe Gossamer Ring.

Halo

Main Ring

Amalthea Gossamer Ring

Thebe Gossamer Ring

Io

Europa

Ganymede

Callisto

A long time ago, Galileo
Galilei used his telescope
to see the movement of the
planets. He also discovered
the 4 largest moons of Jupiter.
They are called the Galilean Moons.

Galilean Moons

This is a painting of what scientist believe it would be like to stand on Europa, the fourth-largest moon of Jupiter, and the smallest of the Galilean moons. Europa may have a vast ocean under its crust. Researchers believe it would be a good place to look for extraterrestrial life.

Saturn

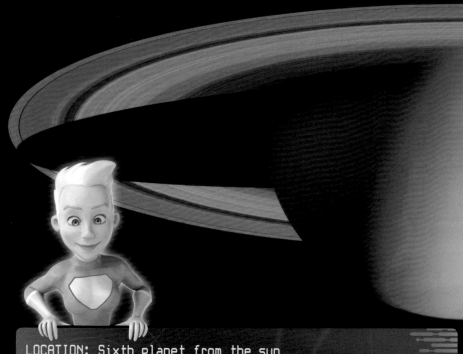

LOCATION: Sixth planet from the sun

TIME TO CIRCLE THE SUN: almost 30 years

NUMBER OF MOONS: 62

CAN HUMANS LIVE HERE: No

TIME FOR SUNLIGHT TO REACH THE PLANET: 1.3 hours

DISTANCE FROM THE SUN: 1.4 billion kilometers (average)
886 million miles (average)

AVERAGE SURFACE TEMPERATURE: Very cold! (-178 °C) (-288 °F)

GRAVITY: Similar to Earth. 45 kilograms (100 pounds)
on Earth is 49 kilograms (107 pounds) on Saturn.

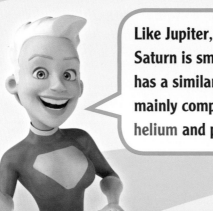

Like Jupiter, Saturn is a gas giant. Saturn is smaller than Jupiter, but it has a similar composition. Saturn is mainly composed of hydrogen and helium and probably has a solid core.

Hydrogen Gas

Hydrogen Liquid

Helium Rain

Ices

Rocky Core

Metallic Hydrogen
and Helium

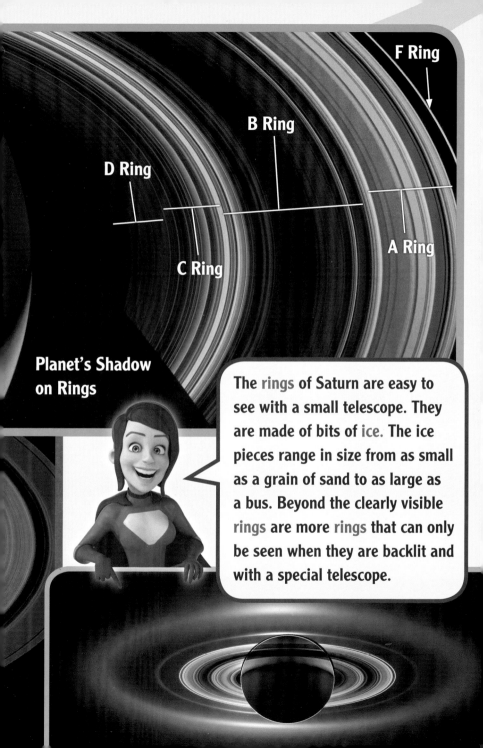

F Ring

B Ring

D Ring

A Ring

C Ring

Planet's Shadow
on Rings

The rings of Saturn are easy to see with a small telescope. They are made of bits of ice. The ice pieces range in size from as small as a grain of sand to as large as a bus. Beyond the clearly visible rings are more rings that can only be seen when they are backlit and with a special telescope.

Janus

Mimas

Titan

Saturn's moons vary greatly in size and shape. **Titan** is Saturn's largest moon, and the second largest moon in the Solar System. This photograph of Saturn shows 6 of Saturn's **62** moons.

Saturn's Moons

Pandora

Epimetheus

Enceladus

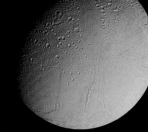

Titan

Epimetheus

Rings

Titan

Titan is a very large moon. It is bigger than the planet Mercury! Here is Titan behind the rings of Saturn and the much smaller moon Epimetheus.

The *Huygens* probe landed on Titan and took this picture of the surface.

Titan is the only moon in the Solar System known to have a full atmosphere. Many scientists want to send more probes to this moon because they think single-celled organisms might be able to live there. So far, however, scientists have found no evidence of life on Titan.

High-Pressure Ice

Liquid Water Ocean

Ice

Rocky Surface

Solid Core

Atmosphere

Uranus

Uranus is unusual because the planet, its rings and its moons appear to be sideways! Scientists think that when the planet and moons were nearly formed, it collided with several large objects, causing everything to tilt.

LOCATION: Seventh planet from the sun

TIME TO CIRCLE THE SUN: about 84 years

NUMBER OF MOONS: 27

CAN HUMANS LIVE HERE: No

TIME FOR SUNLIGHT TO REACH THE PLANET: 2.6 hours

DISTANCE FROM THE SUN: 2.8 billion kilometers (average)
1.8 billion miles (average)

AVERAGE SURFACE TEMPERATURE: Very cold! (-216 °C) (-357 °F)

GRAVITY: Similar to Earth. 45 kilograms (100 pounds) on Earth is 41 kilograms (91 pounds) on Uranus.

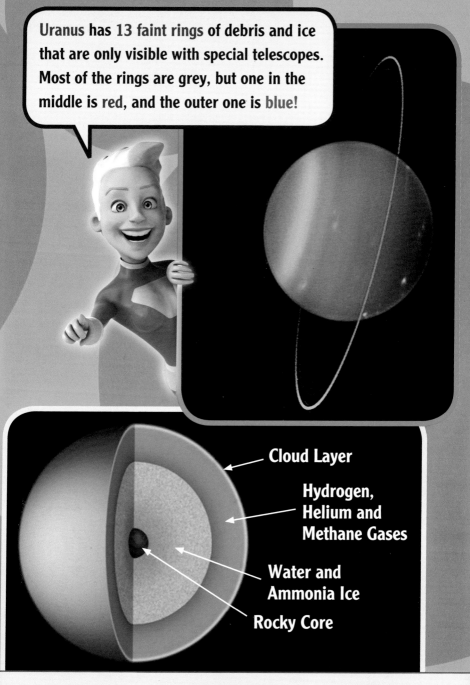

Uranus has 13 faint rings of debris and ice that are only visible with special telescopes. Most of the rings are grey, but one in the middle is red, and the outer one is blue!

Cloud Layer

Hydrogen, Helium and Methane Gases

Water and Ammonia Ice

Rocky Core

Uranus is an ice giant. It has more ice than a gas giant.

Moons of Uranus

Uranus has **27 moons**, all of which were named after characters in the works of Shakespeare. This image of Uranus shows several of its moons.

Umbriel

Titania

Miranda

Ariel

Oberon

These are the 5 main moons of Uranus. They are all made of about equal parts rock and ice. Miranda has the most uneven surface of any object in the solar system!

Neptune

Neptune is the farthest planet from the sun. It is named after the Roman god of the sea. Neptune is the only planet in the solar system that wasn't discovered by seeing it. An astronomer predicted that a big planet must exist beyond Uranus because of how Uranus's orbit varied. Twenty years later, in 1846, Neptune was found by telescope.

LOCATION: Eighth planet from the sun

TIME TO CIRCLE THE SUN: almost 165 years

NUMBER OF MOONS: 14

CAN HUMANS LIVE HERE: No

TIME FOR SUNLIGHT TO REACH THE PLANET: 4.1 hours

DISTANCE FROM THE SUN: 4.5 billion kilometers (average)
                      2.8 billion miles (average)

AVERAGE SURFACE TEMPERATURE: VERY COLD! (-216 °C) (-357 °F)

GRAVITY: Similar to Earth. 45 kilograms (100 pounds) on Earth is 41 kilograms (91 pounds) on Uranus.

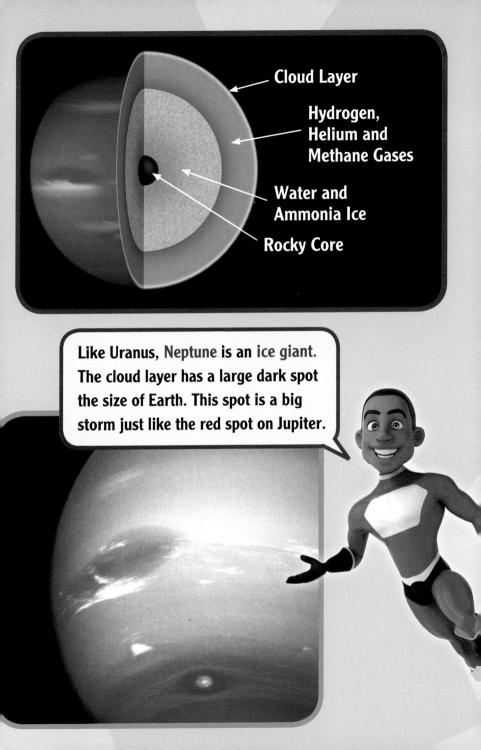

Cloud Layer

Hydrogen, Helium and Methane Gases

Water and Ammonia Ice

Rocky Core

Like Uranus, Neptune is an ice giant. The cloud layer has a large dark spot the size of Earth. This spot is a big storm just like the red spot on Jupiter.

Neptune's Moons & Rings

This photo of Neptune shows 3 of its moons!

Proteus

Despina

Larissa

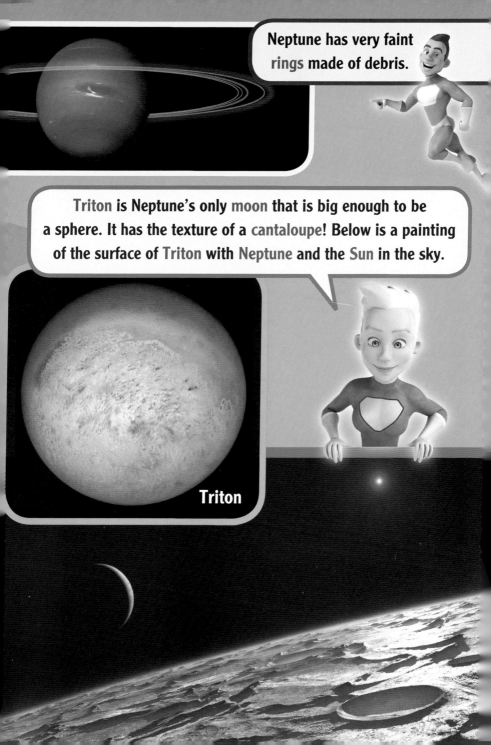

Neptune has very faint rings made of debris.

Triton is Neptune's only moon that is big enough to be a sphere. It has the texture of a cantaloupe! Below is a painting of the surface of Triton with Neptune and the Sun in the sky.

Triton

Dwarf planets are similar to planets. They are round and orbit the Sun. Unlike true planets, dwarf planets are quite small and share their orbit with asteroids. This is a photo of Pluto. Although it was once called a planet, it is now considered a dwarf planet. Pluto has 5 moons!

Pluto

Ceres

Ceres is a dwarf planet between Mars and Jupiter. It orbits the Sun as part of the Main Asteroid Belt.

So far, there are only 5 official dwarf planets, Ceres, Pluto, Eris, Makemake and Haumea. Several round objects close to Pluto may soon be classified as dwarf planets. Astronomers think there may be hundreds of dwarf planets still to be found in our Solar System.

Eris

Dwarf Planets

Pluto's moon, Charon, is such a large moon that some astronomers call the two a double-dwarf planet.

Charon is a little more than half the size of Pluto, and it is made of ice and rock. This is a painting of the surface of Charon, with Pluto as a crescent and the Sun in the distance.

Dysnomia is Eris's only moon. In Greek mythology, Dysnomia is the daughter of the Greek goddess Eris. Detecting moons of dwarf planets is hard because they are so small. Astronomers think that more will be found as telescopes become more powerful.

Dwarf Planet Moons

Asteroids are sometimes called minor planets. Asteroids are smaller and not as round as planets. Like planets, asteroids can have moons!

This asteroid, named Ida, has a tiny moon. Its moon is named Dactyl. Ida is named after a mountain in Greek mythology, and Dactyls were mythical beings that lived on the mountain.

Asteroids are made of rock and minerals, and they have unusual shapes. Like planets, asteroids orbit the Sun. There are more than a million asteroids in our Solar System.

Asteroids

An exoplanet is any planet outside of our Solar System. The first confirmed discovery of an exoplanet was in 1992. Now astronomers have detected several thousand exoplanets. Even though we don't have photographs of exoplanets, artists have painted pictures of what we imagine they look like.

Exoplanets

In the search for exoplanets, astronomers look for planets in the habitable zone—the distance from a star that allows for liquid water. The year 2017 was an excellent year for exoplanet discovery, with several found to be in the habitable zone of their stars.

Life Beyond Earth?

When people think of alien life, they usually imagine strange green creatures. However, the most likely life beyond earth will be single-celled creatures. Nevertheless, astronomers are always looking for radio signals, one of the likely signs of intelligent life.

Geysers on Enceladus

The most likely place to find extraterrestrial life might be Enceladus, one of Saturn's moons. It has geysers of water ice, indicating that liquid water may be found under the surface. Life as we know it requires water to survive.

Printed in China

The Publisher: Super Explorers is an imprint of Blue Bike Books

Library and Archives Canada Cataloguing in Publication

Hartson, Tamara, 1974–, author
    Planets / Tamara Hartson.

Issued in print and electronic formats.
ISBN 978-1-926700-88-5 (softcover).—ISBN 978-1-926700-89-2 (EPUB)

1. Planets—Juvenile literature. 2. Solar system—Juvenile literature.
3. Astronomy—Juvenile literature. 4. Outer space—Juvenile literature.
I. Title.

| QB602.H375 2018 | j523.4 | C2017-907088-6 |
| | | C2017-907089-4 |

Front cover credit: Out of the Dust, A Planet is Born, NASA.

Back cover credits: NASA.

Photo Credits: All photos are courtesy of NASA except for the following: From Wikimedia: Brocken Inaglory 13b; ESO 53c, 55b; ESA/MPS/DLR/IDA 13a; Kelvinsong 45; NASA/JPL-Caltech 2b; NASA National Space Science Data Center/Harvard Micro Observatory/Don P. Mitchell 12bc. From Thinkstock: Cappan 60b; Dance60 9a; PeterHermesFurian 16b; RomoloTavani 2-3; SalvagorGali 17a; Sebastian Kaulitzki 7; shihina 17b; Stockbyte 19b; themotioncloud 10-11; vjanez 30-31.

Superhero Illustrations: julos/Thinkstock.

Produced with the assistance of the Government of Alberta. *Alberta*
Government

We acknowledge the financial support of the Government of Canada.
Nous reconnaissons l'appui financier du gouvernement du Canada.

Funded by the Government of Canada | **Canadä**
Financé par le gouvernement du Canada

PC: 38